Women of Discovery

Five Super Stories of Fab Females Who Made Scientific History

Nury Vittachi
Illustrations by Step Cheung

Contents

The Girl Who Found Her Sisters on the Other Side of the World
Harriet Noyes

The First Woman Doctor in History
Merit Ptah

The Girl Who Had to Hide Behind a Man's Name
Sophie Germain

The Murderous Princess Who Found Salvation
Anna Of Byzantium

The Bug Hunter Who Dreamed of the Jungle
Maria Merian

THE GIRL WHO FOUND HER SISTERS ON THE OTHER SIDE OF THE WORLD

A GIRL AGED 13, sitting in a church in the USA, had a curious feeling. She felt that her destiny was to do something on the other side of the world.

In those days, the 1870s, young women weren't supposed to be interested in travel or work — only in finding a husband.

But the feeling never left Harriet Newell Noyes, and all through her teens and early 20s, she wondered what that special job would be, and what sort of family she would end up with.

When she was 24, she packed her bags and got on a ship to travel to China.

Although she was supposed to be there as a missionary, Harriet had her own motto: "Actions speak louder than words." She would not tell people to live a life of serving others — she would just live such a life herself, and let people see what it was like.

The first thing she realized when she got to Guangzhou was that her sisters in China had it tough. They got very little education. There were many traditions in society that made sure they had no power, and the worst thing of all: their feet were often painfully bound into tiny packages.

She decided that that was her job — she was going to change all this. But how could one woman, from so far away, have any affect?

It seemed impossible.

But Harriet knew that actions speak louder than words, right? So she started small, with a tiny, free school for women called True Light Seminary, the first girls-only college in the city. She started with only six students, but she persevered, and the operation soon began to grow.

If the women had no money, she provided free meals. If they had nowhere to sleep, she gave them bedrooms.

And gently, gently, she persuaded them that foot-binding was a bad thing — and they should unwrap their feet before it was too late.

As the years went by, Harriet's school became a place of miracles — she taught science, mathematics and many other subjects, and the school produced dozens of nurses, more than a hundred doctors, and almost 300 teachers — all female, and all just as good as the men, or better.

The women who unbound their feet told the others how good it felt, and soon, all the women at True Light had normal, healthy feet.

Twenty years after Harriet had started unwrapping the girls' feet, much of Chinese society was discussing the issue. And the government of that period, the Qing Dynasty, passed a law recognizing that feet-binding was evil and was banned forevermore.

Harriet had played a small part in achieving a miracle for her sisters on the other side of the world — and they could all, quite literally, dance for joy.

THE FIRST WOMAN DOCTOR IN HISTORY

SOME PEOPLE THINK THAT it's only recently that women have been allowed to become doctors. But historians know that there was already a famous woman doctor in 2700 BC, more than four millennia ago, at the dawn of recorded history.

Her name was Merit Ptah and she lived in Egypt. She is the first named female doctor in history, and may also be the earliest named woman scientist of any kind.

The "Pt" in her name is the same "pt" that you see in the word Egypt. The place name comes from the ancient word Hikuptah, which means "Home of the Soul of Ptah".

Merit Ptah was named after the god Ptah, who is said to have created reality with a thought.

That is kind of cool, because modern scientists say there seems to be some mysterious connection between thoughts (in the form of the taking of conscious measurements) and the physical reality of the particles which make up everything. (If you are interested in that idea, look up "measurement problem" and "quantum physics".)

This interpretation of quantum physics indicates that matter seems to be made of ideas, as a famous scientist called Werner Heisenberg said, so perhaps reality really is a thought in the mind of someone. But we don't know if his or her name is Ptah!

How do we know about this early doctor, who lived long before most examples of written history?

A picture of her was found in a tomb in a pyramid, with a piece of text written by her son, a High Priest. He says his mother is "the Chief Physician", which suggests that she was a top doctor with others under her command.

Merit Ptah's existence shows that even in the early days of human history, women could have really important jobs, as they should.

She's important — so in modern times, when astronomers were looking for names to use on landmarks on other planets, they gave her name to a crater on the planet Venus, calling it the Merit Ptah crater.

If you grow up to be an inter-planetary explorer, and end up on the planet Venus, I hope you'll remember this tale. You'll be able to tell your friends: "This crater is named after Merit Ptah, the earliest named female scientist in history."

THE GIRL WHO HAD TO HIDE BEHIND A MAN'S NAME

SOPHIE WAS FORBIDDEN from leaving the house. Again! Not fair. For weeks, she had been made to stay indoors.

Why? Sophie Germain, aged 13, lived in a country and a time where bad government had made many people angry. There was fighting in the streets, so she had to say inside for safety. Boring!

What could she do? This was in France in 1789, so there were no computers or Internet or television or any such modern entertainments — not even a radio.

But there was one bright spot in her life. Her father had created a library in his house — and she made herself at home in the room full of books, and was soon lost in her own, an armchair traveler in a world of words.

You'd think her parents would be happy, but no. They expected Sophie Germain to read "girl" books, educational ones about art and music and languages.

But Sophie went straight for what her family considered "boy" books, and her favorites were the most unlikely ones of all (so her parents thought): those on mathematics.

She was particularly enchanted by reading about Archimedes. He was a Greek mathematician, and many of the important equations we use to build everything from bridges to buildings came from him. A lot of people don't realize that without maths we would not have anything that is engineered — no buildings, no machines, no computers.

One of the history books said that when a Roman soldier killed Archimedes in a battle, the old mathematician's last words referred to the geometry papers he was carrying — "Do not disturb the circles." Mathematics is important!

On dark winter evenings, Sophie would go to her bedroom and stay up late writing equations. Her parents were angry, and took away her room-heater and her coats, so that she would be too cold to work.

Sophie wrapped her blanket around her and worked on the equations she was learning by candlelight.

One morning, her mother found her asleep at her desk on a day so cold that the ink had frozen in her inkwell.

From that time, her mother secretly helped her.

Sophie Germain grew up to become a great mathematician, although she signed much of her work using a male name "Monsieur LeBlanc".

She made important progress on a very famous puzzle called Fermat's Last Theorem, that had mathematicians around the world stumped.

One of her great achievements was to create a formula to work out the elasticity, or bendiness, of materials. This meant that engineers could build high structures without fearing that they would break into pieces.

After her death, the Eiffel Tower was built, partly using her calculations. The builders wrote the names of 72 scientists on the tower, but did not put her name on the list, probably because she was a woman.

Next time you see a picture of the Eiffel Tower in France, remember the girl whose name is not on it: the girl who had to stay at home every night — but then discovered her father's library and started traveling in her mind.

THE MURDEROUS PRINCESS WHO FOUND SALVATION

DID YOU HEAR ABOUT the evil princess who tried to kill her brother?

True story: Once there was a girl called Anna of Byzantium, aged 14. More than anything, she wanted to make history.

She seemed to be in a good position to do so, as she had been born into one of the richest and most powerful families in the Mediterranean.

But in those days, and this was almost 1,000 years ago, being a princess was tough. Princesses were used as tools to join families together.

While she was a baby, a husband had been chosen for her. But he died while she was still a child.

STEP C.

When Anna (full name Anna Komnene) was 14, another husband was chosen for her: a young leader named Caesar Nikephoros Bryennios the Younger. She agreed — no choice, really. (The two of them seemed to get on well, and eventually had four children.)

But Anna was ambitious and hardworking, and her parents allowed her to be educated in astronomy, mathematics, and (her favorite subject) philosophy, which her teacher said was "the queen of all sciences".

When she became a young woman, her father put her in charge of a hospital, where she learned about life and death and thousands of different types of medicine. She became quite the scientist.

But when her father had more children, and one was a boy, sexism reared its ugly head. It was decreed that he should become the next leader of the land, because even though she was the oldest child, she was just a girl.

And when her dad died, that's what happened.

Anna felt strongly that she and her husband should become the leaders. So she set up a plot to kill her own younger brother.

But to her amazement, her husband refused to help, and eventually the plot was exposed. Her younger brother, who was now king, took away all the land and money belonging to his sister and her husband and exiled them.

Anna complained that since women were supposed to be softer-hearted than men, God must have accidentally given her and her husband each other's genders!

Then her luck turned even worse.

Her husband died, and she had nowhere to go except to a convent where she would live as a nun until she died.

It seemed like really bad news — but it turned out to be the best thing that could have happened.

As a nun, living in a quiet place where she could think about the important things in life, she finally became a person of worth. Her life, full of rich and powerful experiences, and all that time she had spent in a hospital, and the twists and turns of her life, meant that she had acquired a measure of wisdom.

At the age of 55, she decided to finish writing a book of history and science that her husband had started. It ended up as a 15-volume book called "The Alexiad", containing important knowledge about that period of history, a time in Europe sometimes known as "the dark ages".

Anna of Byzantium, the evil princess who tried to murder her brother, became a good nun and an early science writer — and finally found herself a place in history.

THE BUG HUNTER WHO DREAMED OF THE JUNGLE

GIRLS DON'T LIKE BUGS, RIGHT? Wrong! The truth is that one of the world's greatest bug scientists was a woman. And she started young.

Maria Merian was 13 when she started painting insects. She was particularly intrigued that ugly creatures that looked like horrible maggots could turn into beautiful butterflies.

It was an odd interest for a girl in those days, but she loved knowledge. Her father had been a publisher, so she had been born into a house of books, in 1647 in the city of Frankfurt, Germany.

But he had died when she was three.

Then her mother had married a painter, and the child had learned to paint from watching her stepfather.

She soon realized that she could combine her interest in insects with her father's skill in book production and her stepfather's skill in painting to create books of nature pictures.

But how could she get people interested in bugs?

She knew what to do — she would have to travel to an exotic distant jungle and find GIANT bugs — insects so big and scary that they could eat birds!

But of course, real life is never as exciting as your dream, is it? Her life took a rather boringly normal path. Maria Merian grew up, got married, and had children — and would sometimes sigh. Would she ever get a chance to make her dream come true?

One day, she decided that she had to go back to her original dream, and she made the break. She sold 255 of her paintings to raise money, and then set sail on a ship to do a scientific investigation of the insects of a land called Suriname, which is in South America.

She took with her one of her children, 19-year-old Dorothea, plus her notebooks and paints.

Some people say that her trip might be the first real science-focused expedition. (Before that, scientists just took a cabin on ships transporting goods or tourists.)

STEP C.

After weeks of travel, Maria Merian and her daughter entered the jungles of Suriname. They saw lots of amazing things and discovered new animals and plants. Maria painted a spider so big that it could capture and eat a bird — something that would amaze her readers, who could never have imagined such a thing.

They spent two years there before returning to Europe. Maria produced lots of paintings and books. One of them, published after her death, was called "The Caterpillars' Marvelous Transformation and Strange Floral Food".

Have you seen any of those famous BBC TV documentaries about animals? The man who made those, David Attenborough, said Maria Merian was one of the world's most important naturalists in the area of small creatures.

And recently, on what would have been her 366th birthday, Google dressed up its search page with a Merian-style picture of a young iguana (its tail made the second "g" in Google).

So don't let anyone tell you that girls can't cope with bugs! Maria Merian introduced the world to some of the biggest and scariest bugs of all.

KEEP READING

READING ABOUT THE LIVES of scientists and other discoverers adds to our store of knowledge, but we hope also leads us towards something much greater, which is wisdom.

This book is part of a series, which we hope you'll enjoy reading, and will spur you on to do your own scientific research.

The creators of this book wish you success in your explorations.

THE YOUNG SCIENTISTS SERIES

Book 1: SECRETS IN THE ROCKS
Five Astounding Tales of People Solving Mysteries Beneath Our Feet

Book 2: FABULOUS PHYSICS
Five Amazing Stories of People Who Solved Nature's Puzzles

Book 3: MAGICAL MATHEMATICS
Five Astonishing Stories of People Who Did Miracles with Numbers

Book 4: BREAKERS OF BARRIERS
Five Stunning Stories of People Demolishing Walls to Make History

Book 5: SCIENTIFIC PIONEERS
Five Incredible Tales of People Who Helped Develop the Scientific Method

Book 6: THE AMAZING QUANTUM
Five Awesome Stories of People Who Made a Revolution in Physics

Book 7: THE SCIENCE OF HUMANITY
Five Fascinating Stories of People Who Helped Us Understand Ourselves

Book 8: WOMEN OF DISCOVERY
Five Super Stories of Fabulous Females Who Made Scientific History

Book 9: THE INVENTOR'S SPARK
Five Marvelous Stories of People Who Helped Shape the Modern World

Book 10: ADVANCES IN ALCHEMY
Five Startling Stories of Chemistry and Biology

Book 11: THE CALL OF THE STARS
Five Wonderful Stories of People Looking to the Heavens

Book 12: MYSTERIES OF NATURE'S LAWS
Five Striking Stories of People Investigating the Deepest Puzzles of Reality

Published by

WS Education, an imprint of
World Scientific Publishing Co. Pte. Ltd.
5 Toh Tuck Link, Singapore 596224
USA office: 27 Warren Street, Suite 401-402, Hackensack, NJ 07601
UK office: 57 Shelton Street, Covent Garden, London WC2H 9HE

National Library Board, Singapore Cataloguing in Publication Data
Name(s): Vittachi, Nury, 1958– | Cheung, Step, illustrator.
Title: Women of discovery : five super stories of fabulous females who made scientific history / author, Nury Vittachi ; illustrator, Step Cheung.
Other title(s): Young scientists series ; 8.
Description: Singapore : World Scientific Publishing Co Pte Ltd, 2017.
Identifier(s): OCN 969705440 | ISBN 978-981-3221-60-4 (paperback)
Subject(s): LCSH: Women scientists--Juvenile literature. | Women in science--Juvenile literature. | Science--Juvenile literature.
Classification: DDC 509.252--dc23

British Library Cataloguing-in-Publication Data
A catalogue record for this book is available from the British Library.

All royalties received will be channelled to the National Book Development Council of Singapore (NBDCS) as a gift from the author.

First published 2017
Reprinted 2018

Printed in Singapore